Vintage Angels

Christmas coloring book for adults relaxation

Christmas quiet coloring book

Copyright © 2019 by Color me Vintage

More Christmas Coloring Books
By Color Me vintage:

More Christmas Coloring Books
By Color Me vintage:

Also by Color me Vintage:

Join us @ Facebook
Twitter
Pinterest

www.ingramcontent.com/pod-product-compliance
Lightning Source LLC
LaVergne TN
LVHW060221080526
838202LV00052B/4321